DEADLY MISSION

CANADIAN AIRMEN OVER NUREMBERG MARCH 30TH/31ST 1944

by
Dr. W. Rodney, DFC & Bar

Access to History No. 8

**CEF BOOKS
2001**

© William Rodney 2001
All rights reserved. No part of this work covered by copyright herein may be reproduced or used in any form - graphic, electronic, or mechanical, without the prior written permission of the publisher.

National Library of Canada Cataloguing in Publication Data
Rodney, W., 1922-
   Deadly mission: Canadian airmen over Nuremberg, March 30th/31st, 1944
(Access to history series; no. 8)
Includes bibliographical references.
ISBN 1-896979-42-4

   1. Nuremberg (Germany)—History—Bombardment, 1944- 2. World War, 1939-1945—Aerial Operations, Canadian. 3. Great Britain. Royal Air Force. Bomber Command. I. Title. II. Series.
D757.9.N8R63 2001   940.54'213324   C2001-902389-8

Published by:
   CEF BOOKS
   PO BOX 40083,
   OTTAWA, ONTARIO K1V 0W8
   613-823-7000

This book is dedicated to the memory of the 110,000 Canadians who willingly gave their lives in the defence of freedom in the Twentieth Century.
   Lest We Forget

Acknowledgements:
   We would like to thank Ontario Command of The Royal Canadian Legion, in particular Mr.Earl Kish, and the Department of Canadian Heritage for the support which made this series possible. Additional thanks to Mr. Jim Moffat for his valuable contribution to this book.

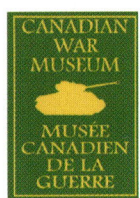

Publication of this book has been supported by the Canadian War Museum.

Front cover: Halifax over a French Target, 1944 (DND/PL32846)
Back cover: Night Target, Germany, 1946 by Miller Brittain (CWM 10889)

High Flight

Oh, I have slipped the surly bonds of earth,
And danced the skies on laughter-silvered wings;
Sunward I've climbed and joined the tumbling mirth
Of sun-split clouds - and done a hundred things
You have not dreamed of - wheeled and soared and swung
High in the sunlit silence. Hov'ring there,
I've chased the shouting wind along and flung
My eager craft through footless halls of air.
Up, up the long delirious, burning blue
I've topped the wind-swept heights with easy grace,
Where never lark, or even eagle, flew;
And, while with silent, lifting mind I've trod
The high untrespassed sanctity of space,
Put out my hand, and touched the face of God.

    Pilot Officer John Gillespie Magee,
    Royal Canadian Air Force
    Killed December 11th, 1941. Age 19.

Table of Contents

Introduction 1

The War to March 1944 3

Bomber Command 4
    The Organization of Bomber Command 4
    The "Boys" of Bomber Command 6
    The British Commonwealth Air Training Plan 6
    Overseas 7
    On Operations 8

Tactics and Technology of the Air War 8
    Early Tactics 9
    Electronic Aids and Radar 9
    Opposing Aircraft 12
    Evasive Tactics 15
    The German Defences 16
    German Fighter Tactics 16

The Nuremberg Raid, March 30th/31st, 1944 19
    The Target 19
    The Route 21
    The Main Force 27
    The Mission 29

Nuremberg - The Analysis 36

Bibliography - Suggested Reading 41

Canada's Roll of Honour, March 30th/31st, 1944 42

Air Raid on San Giusto, Pisa by Paul Goranson (CWM 11435)

Introduction

As darkness fell on March 30th, 1944, more than a thousand Allied aircraft took off from airfields across England. Their mission was to fly 1,000 km from their bases, over occupied Europe, and deliver almost 3,000 tonnes of high-explosive and incendiary bombs on the unsuspecting German City of Nuremberg. In the deafening roar of the stream of 900 bombers were 6,493 airmen from all across the British Commonwealth; Australia, New Zealand, South Africa, Britain and Rhodesia. Almost 1,500 of them were Canadians.

The mission was to be like others in the air war over Europe, a war of a thousand battles, fought continuously over five years. It was another raid into the heartland of Nazi Europe, another strike at Hitler's Fortress, another mission in the Strategic Bomber Offensive and another night for the "Boys" of Bomber Command.

It was a mission to destroy another German city to destroy, with its factories, plants and railways. Many cities had already felt the wrath of Bomber Command and been dealt the consequences of Hitler's war of aggression: Berlin, Hamburg, Dresden, Lubeck to name only a few. Now Nuremberg, the heart of the Nazis, home of the great Rallies that contributed so much to the war, was the target.

In the dark, clear skies over northern Europe, a sky well-lit by a bright moon, the Boys of Bomber Command moved closer to Nuremberg; but on this night luck would not be with them, and in the moonlight German nightfighters would extract a bloody cost for the Raid. For many of the crews this was to be their last flight. One in ten would not make it back.

The Strategic Bomber Offensive was one of the most controversial campaigns in the entire Second World War. Today it is hard to imagine the reasons for bombing cities when it is known thousands of civilians, women and children, would die, but to judge the circumstances of 1944 you have to understand the times in which the decision was made. First, the Second World War was the most horrible war fought in the history of mankind. The atrocities committed on the people of Europe by Adolf Hitler, the mass murders, the extermination of millions, were beyond the comprehension of a normal person. Secondly, from 1939 to 1943, Hitler had been very close to winning the war. His Armies had conquered Europe and were close to defeating the Russians. Desperate situations call for desperate measures, and it is from defeat that Bomber Command was born. Brutality is a part of war and when fighting against the most cruel of enemies there can be no quarter. They must be stopped at all costs. It is your people or theirs. There is no high moral road in total war.

Another argument is whether the result of the Strategic Bomber Offensive was a success or worth the price paid. This is difficult to decide, as historians can present both sides using their own statistics; however it is hard to imagine the leveling of cities and factories not having some effect on the production of war material and the morale of the Germans. What is clear and important to the outcome of the Second World War, is that had the thousands of anti-aircraft guns, fighter aircraft and pilots needed to protect the cities from the bombers been deployed against Allied soldiers and tanks in Italy, Russia or in Normandy, the tide of war might have been reversed.

Beyond the historical arguments, the real picture is of the brave men in the bombers, men who knew the odds of survival were not good, but chose to risk their lives to stop Adolf Hitler. In the moon-lit skies en route to Nuremberg that night of March 30th, 1944, many a brave soul would curse this deadly mission.

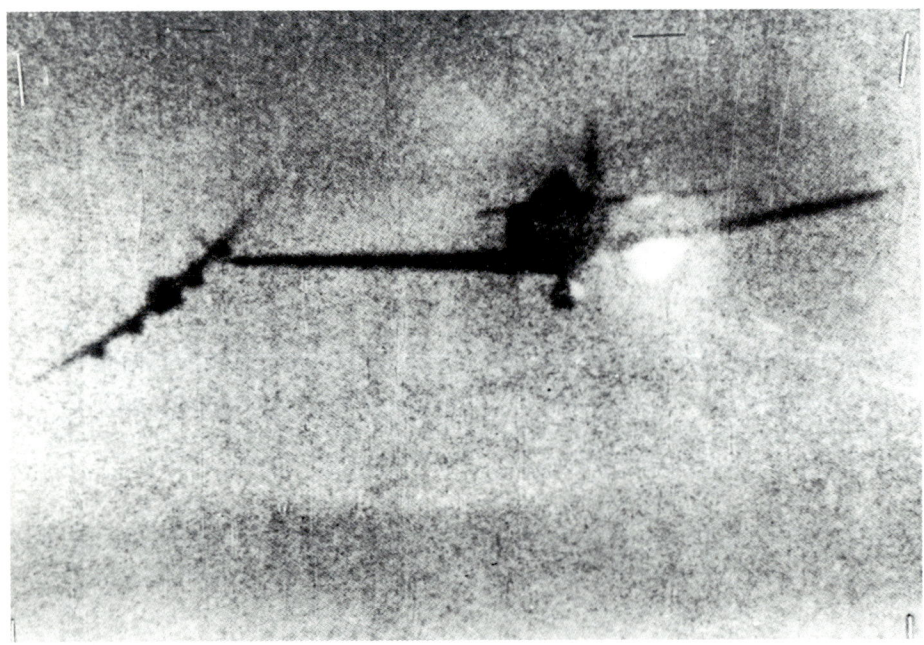

German Focke-Wulf fighter attacking a Lancaster of Bomber Command.

(PA 202786)

The War To March 1944

In September 1939 the Germans invaded Poland and started the Second World War. The Allies were Britain and France and the many members of the British Commonwealth including Canada and Australia. The United States and Soviet Russia were neutral. Italy later joined the Nazis and formed the Axis Powers.

The war was quiet until May 1940 when German soldiers and armour overran and defeated France. The Nazis eventually captured all of Europe, including Holland, Belgium, Denmark, and Norway. In August and September 1940 the Battle of Britain was fought in the skies over southern England. This air battle pitted British fighters against a massive German air attack, in which Nazi bombers dropped tonnes of explosives on the principal British cities and ports, killing thousands of civilians. There can be no doubt that when the time came the Allies would pay the Germans back.

By the end of 1940 Britain, supplied by the convoys which crossed the U-boat infested North Atlantic, was barely hanging on. The war had spread to North Africa and in 1941 Hitler made the fatal mistake of attacking the neutral Soviet Union. By December 1941 the Germans were at the gates of Moscow. Hitler had given the Allies a new partner, Russia. Then on December 7, 1941 the Japanese, a new member of the Axis, attacked American, Dutch and British positions in the Pacific and the Far East. Now the Allies consisted of Britain, its Empire, including Canada, the United States and Soviet Russia.

Into 1942 the war continued to go badly for the Allies. They had been caught off-balance by the Axis attacks and it took some time for them to recover. By the end of 1942 the Germans and Italians had been defeated in North Africa. In Russia the Germans were slowly being ground down in a brutal war of attrition.

In 1943 the Russians crushed a German Army at Stalingrad, and the British, Americans and Canadians conquered Sicily and invaded Italy. In September 1943 Italy surrendered. In the Far East the Japanese were finally stopped.

As 1944 started the tide of war had clearly turned. The Germans were now on the run, but they were in no way defeated. Major battles were being fought on the Russian front. Allied plans were being made for the great invasion of France, but the heartland of Nazi Germany was still far away. Only through Bomber Command could the Allies strike at the heart of the enemy.

Bomber Command

Bomber Command was reorganized and strengthened after the defeat of France in May 1940. Its purpose was to attack industrial targets and its mission became the "Strategic Bomber Offensive". In the early days there were few available aircraft. Those in command felt the bombers were adequately armed to defend themselves against attacking fighters. The air raids were made in daylight with relatively little planning and few navigational aids. The results were heavy losses, missed targets and demoralized aircrew. It was quickly decided that to have successful raids the bombers would have to fly at night and be properly equipped with radar and other navigational aids. To the end of the war there was a constant technological battle between the Allies and Germans to gain an upper hand on navigational technology.

In 1942 Bomber Command received a new chief, Air Chief Marshal Arthur Harris. Sometimes referred to as "Butch" or "Butcher" to the men of Bomber Command, Harris was a single-minded, ruthless proponent of bombing industrial and civilian targets. He felt he could "bring Germany to her knees with bombing" by smashing " systematically principle cities". To Harris the fight in the skies was to be the decisive battle of the war.

The Organization of Bomber Command

Throughout 1943 Bomber Command continued to grow. Bigger and better aircraft were arriving. The four-engined Halifaxes and Lancasters could carry heavier bomb loads, and fly deeper into Germany. New navigational equipment arrived.

By 1944 Bomber Command was divided into seven operational groups based in 54 airfields, less than 250 km apart from just north of London to Yorkshire. There were 76 squadrons of more than 1,000 aircraft of varying types.

Groups One, Three, Four, Five were bombers, mostly Lancasters but some squadrons and Four Group were equipped with Halifax bombers. A host of Nationalities were represented by the squadrons; Poles, Australians, Rhodesians, but the men were primarily British. An individual crew would be made up of any number of different nationalities. The only common thread was that they were all volunteers.

Six Group was made up of 15 Canadian Squadrons including; 408 (Goose), 420 (Snowy Owl), 424 (Tiger), 426 (Thunderbird), 427 (Lion), 428 (Ghost), 425 (Alouette), 429 (Bison) and 433 (Porcupine). They were largely manned by Canadians, however, at the time of the Nuremberg raid, many aircrew, particularly flight engineers, were still drawn from the Royal Air Force.

DEADLY MISSION

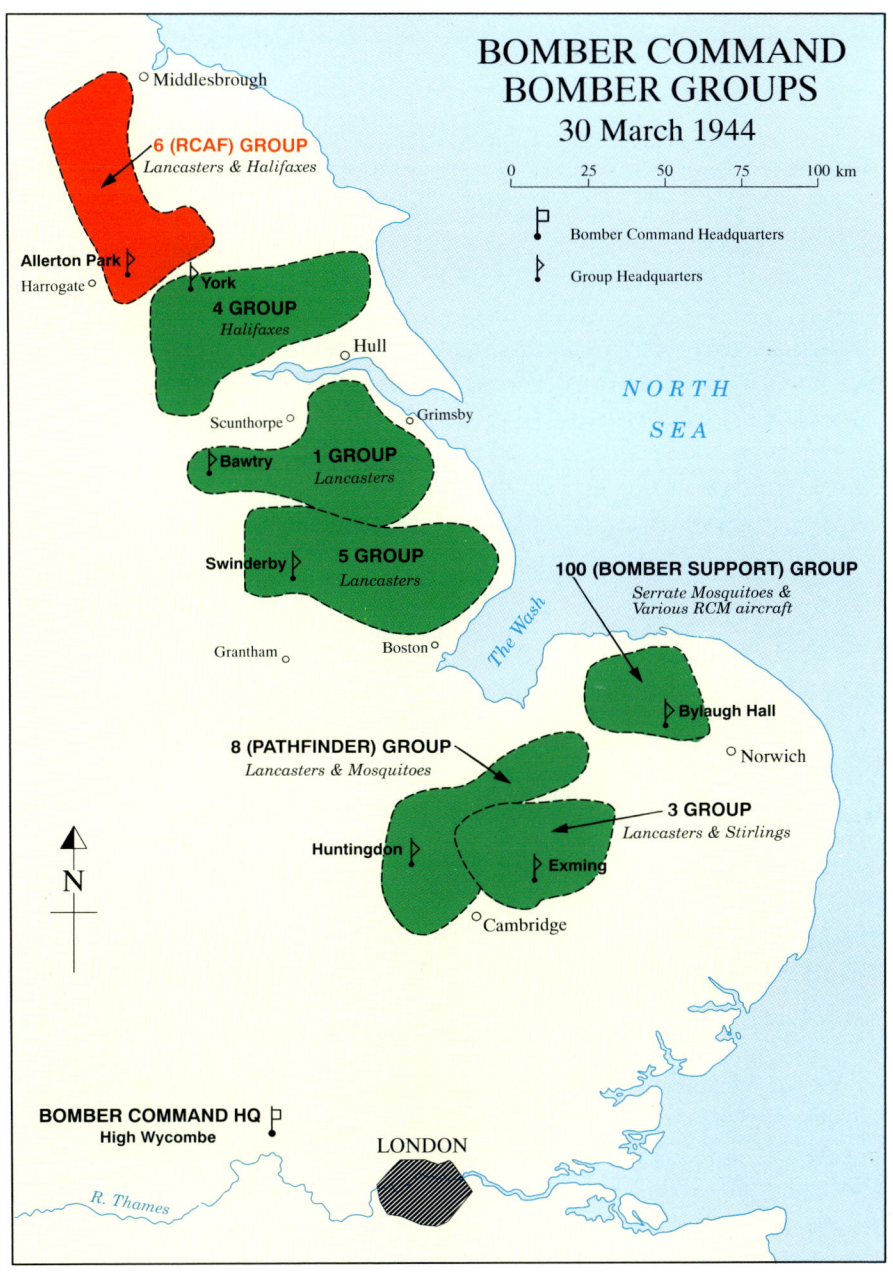

CANADIAN AIRMEN OVER NUREMBERG

In March 1944 probably a third of Six Group were not Canadian and there would be more Canadians flying with RAF Groups than in Six Group. These unusual mixtures were a direct result of the British Commonwealth Air Training Program.

There were two other specialist Groups. Number Eight was the Pathfinders (PFF). These squadrons were responsible for marking routes and targets and were indispensable to the success of a bombing raid. Number 100 was a special bomber support Group which had many tasks including supplying night-fighter Intruders.

The "Boys" of Bomber Command

The "Brylcreem boys", as the men in the Air Force were known, were a comparatively well educated group, and drawn from all levels of society. Most began training when they were still in their late teens (18 was not an uncommon age) when they enlisted in the various Commonwealth Air Forces. They were all volunteers and came from every country in the British Empire, the United States or were refugees from German-occupied countries such as Poland, France, Norway or Holland.

They were all flyers, and many trained in Canada under the British Commonwealth Air Training Program (BCATP).

"It drives one mad to think that some Canadian boor, who probably can't even find Europe on the globe, flies here from a country glutted with natural resources which his people don't even know how to exploit, to bombard a continent with a crowded population."
Joseph Goebbels, Nazi Germany's Minister of Propaganda.

British Commonwealth Air Training Program

Although training establishments existed in Australia, Britain, New Zealand and South Africa, the majority of aircrew learned their trades at Canadian (BCATP) bases.

Pilots were the BCATP's centrepiece. Once they passed the physical requirements, in particular proved they had 20/20 vision and were not colour-blind, they went on navigation, wireless, aircraft recognition courses, and had flight simulator experience on the Link trainer at Initial Training Schools (ITS). If successful, there followed postings to Elementary Flying Schools. There they flew deHaviland Tiger Moths, Fairchild Coronells or Fleet Finchs depending upon the station and the stage of the war. Those who succeeded

DEADLY MISSION

acquired some 60 hours of flight experience. The training was rigorous and included aerobatics, spins, instrument flying, together with more time on the Link trainer. Those who failed to solo within 10 or 12 hours were generally "washed-out" and remustered to other aircrew trades.

The successful cadets then proceeded to Service Flying Training Schools (SFTS) where they accumulated roughly 225 hours on the twin-engined Avro Anson or Cessna Crane, or the Harvard. After completing all this, only then did the pilot obtain his most coveted possession, his "wings".

Navigators were, after pilots, the most rigorously trained aircrew. They underwent 16 weeks of airborne training. Training periods for wireless operators, bomb-aimers, and gunners differed in length but each category obtained sufficient flying experience to make crew integration viable and for the most part, an effective process.

Thus prepared, the bomber boys, who had not been diverted to training or staff pilot duties, went overseas.

The BCATP was an enormous success. Between establishment on December 17th, 1939 and 1944 the Training Plan in Canada produced 131,553 Australian, British, Canadian and New Zealand aircrew.

Of the graduates, 72,835 were from the Royal Canadian Air Force. There were 25,747 pilots, 12,855 navigators (including those trained as observers), 6,659 bomb-aimers, 12,744 wireless operator/air gunners, 12,917 air gunners, and 1,913 flight engineers (the majority of flight engineers were trained in Britain). In fact the Program produced so many Canadian aircrew that roughly two-thirds of the Canadians who served overseas in an operational capacity had to serve with Royal Air Force squadrons. Bomber Command absorbed the greatest number of BCATP graduates.

Overseas

Once overseas those destined for Bomber Command underwent further training at Advanced Flying Units (AFU) where they obtained 30 or so more hours of experience mostly on the more demanding Airspeed Oxford.

The next step was the Operational Training Units (OTU), at which the pilots through a seemingly inefficient method of informal conversations and personal contact with navigators, wireless operators, bomb-aimers, and gunners, usually over a few drinks, formed their crews. Because of their common BCATP training it was not uncommon for crews to be composed of men from Britain, Australia, Canada and New Zealand. At OTU the air training would continue. The cadets would fly Vickers Wellington III's and X's and

Armstrong Whitworth Whitleys for approximately 50 hours. Gradually the crews became familiar with the intricacies of operating a heavy aircraft at night using electronic and wireless aids for navigation, and advanced bomb sights for target practice.

The next process was at the Heavy Conversion Units (HCU) where Flight Engineers were added to the crews. Here they accumulated a further 40 hours flying. At the HCU they would fly four-engined Halifax IIs and Xs, Lancaster Is or Short Stirlings.

When a crew finally joined an operational squadron the pilot on average had 400 hours of flying experience, while the rest of the crew members had considerably less.

Now they were ready to fly into battle against an enemy, using superior airborne weapons, good aircraft and sophisticated electronic equipment, with the decided advantage of operating over home territory.

On Operations

After arriving on a Squadron, but before proceeding on operations the crews flew many cross country flights and practiced bombing and generally familiarized themselves with the more advanced aircraft and equipment. In most cases the pilot was sent on an Operation as a co-pilot (known as a "second dickey") with an experienced crew. This way he could observe an experienced crew in action. Then he would be ready to take his own crew over enemy territory.

Survival in the night skies over Germany rested largely on experience, and it was during the first five sorties that losses were the greatest. Nerves for the first Operations were always the worst.

Tactics & Technology of the Air War

The war in the air lasted more than five years during which there were many innovations in bomber tactics and technological breakthroughs. However for each development the Allies made there was always a counter-measure by the enemy. The advantage in the skies changed hands many times. On the night of the Nuremberg Raid, March 30th/31st, 1944, the Germans employed two technical breakthroughs, both unknown to Bomber Command.

Early Tactics

The bombing of civilian targets, including transport centres or industrial facilities by large bi-planes or even Zeppelins was utilized by both sides in the First World War. At the outbreak of the Second World War many thought aerial bombing was to be the great weapon of victory. However the first bomber raids in 1939-1940 were inconsistent and unorganized. In daylight squadrons would take off, fly to the target and drop their bombs on what they saw. The German fighters quickly demonstrated that daylight attacks were costly and Bomber Command switched the raids to night. The next tactical change took place as the Nazis developed a bigger night-fighter force, which could find the attacking bombers using ground and radar equipment. As the attackers were often spread out, they became easy targets, as a one-on-one battle was often won by the fighter. This led to the "Bomber Stream". This was a tight grouping of bombers that attacked in force. It was a well-controlled convoy that followed a designated route to and from the target.

There were no Allied fighters to accompany the bomber stream, as none at the time had the range. The bombers had to protect themselves from the German fighters.

The next development was the special Pathfinder squadrons, whose tasks were to mark the significant points on the route and over the target areas. The Pathfinders used a variety of flares and coloured markers.

On the eve of Nuremberg "Bomber Streams" of up to 1,000 aircraft were attacking at night, without much fighter support, following a set route to and from the objective. The objective was marked by the Pathfinders.

Electronic Aids and Radar

The whole Air War came down to a game of "cat and mouse". The Allies tried to hide the bomber stream, while the Germans tried to find it. To disguise their intentions much use was made of radio signals and radar, by both sides. Each side would come up with new methods to fool the enemy while the enemy would find ways to jam the others Signals.

Throughout the ebb and flow of development and deployment of electronic methods to facilitate navigation, identification of hostile aircraft, and defence, Bomber Command resorted to a variety of tactical and technical innovations in its campaign against Nazi Germany. Amongst the first navigation aides were Gee and Oboe. Gee was the earliest navigational aid and the Germans quickly learned how to jam the signals and therefore its use was limited to the early operations of Bomber Command.

Oboe was based on signals sent from separate transmitters in England and where the two signals intersected was the target. Pathfinder aircraft were equipped to pick up the beams, and therefore bomb accurately. However due to the curvature of the earth, the further away from England you were the higher the altitude required to pick up the waves. Consequently Oboe was not employed against distant targets such as Nuremberg.

Bomber Command's principal electronic navigation aid was H2S or as it was known, "Stinker". H2S was a radar set in the bomber. It had a small screen on which the terrain below was reflected. With the right operator it could give important information about the whereabouts of the aircraft.

The bomber's tactic was to use Gee on the outward-bound legs to confirm positions and determine wind velocities until German jamming masked the transmissions. That generally occurred soon after the bomber stream reached the continent. Consequently the bomber crews used H2S to help pinpoint their positions in order to determine wind velocities at the higher levels. Accurately determining the winds was a critical part of a raid. Should the winds spread out the bomber stream, they would be easy targets for the German night-fighters. To accurately gauge the winds, the H2S findings, together with results transmitted every half-hour from lead bombers, known as the Zephyr system, were intended to keep the bomber stream together.

The object of all the navigational aids was to get the maximum number of aircraft to and through the target in minimum time, and to minimize the possibilities of airborne interceptions. The problem was that the German Air Force or Luftwaffe, could pick up on the H2S signals and find the bomber stream that way. The great number of Bomber Command aircraft involved in a raid made tracking the stream relatively easy for German ground radar installations. The wholesale use of H2S by the RAF crews during operations maximized the possibilities of interception by night fighters.

The Germans were no fools and they quickly developed airborne electronic aids to nullify the Allies' advances. They produced a number of their own counter-measures, such as *Flensburg, SN - 2, or Naxos.*

Window was a surprising successful development by the RAF, that for a brief period gave Bomber Command an advantage. Window was strips of aluminum that would be dropped by the millions by bombers that would wreak havoc with the Nazi communications. For a few months in 1943, particularly when bombing Hamburg, Window was the advantage. But once again the Germans developed a system, known as SN-2, that could see through Window. On the night of the Nuremberg Raid many German fighters were equipped with SN-2.

DEADLY MISSION

Marshalling the Hallies by Paul Goranson (CWM 11402)

Opposing Aircraft

The Lancaster
The Avro Lancaster was the premier RAF bomber in 1944. It was four-engined, with a maximum speed exceeding 450 km/hour, a range of 2800 km with a 5440 kg bomb load, and a ceiling of 5800 metres. The "Lanc" could carry a bomb load of up to 8200 kg. Its armament was two machine-guns (.303) in the nose, two machine-guns in the dorsal turret and four machine-guns in the tail turret. It had a crew of seven.

The Halifax
The Halifaxes were being replaced by the quicker Lancasters in 1944, but many were still around for the Nuremberg Raid. It was four-engined, with a maximum speed of 450 km/hour, a range of 3200 km with a bomb load of 3200 kg, and a ceiling of 7400 metres. The "Hally Bag" could carry a maximum bomb load of 6600 kg. Its armament was similar to that of the Lancaster, and it also had a crew of seven.

Messerschmitt 110
The Me110 was the Luftwaffe's premier night-fighter. It had a maximum speed of 550 km/hour, a range of 1300 km and a ceiling of 8000 metres. Its armament consisted of two 30 mm cannon in the nose, two 20 mm cannon in the ventral tray, and one 7.92 mm machine-gun in the dorsal position. If outfitted for shrage musik, it had two 20 mm cannon in the rear fuselage. It had a crew of two.

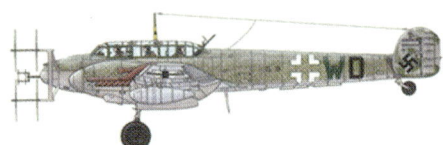

Junkers Ju88
The Ju88 was a night fighter with a crew of four. It had a maximum speed of 626 km/hour, a range of 2250 km, and a ceiling of 10,000 metres. Its armament consisted of four 20 mm cannon in the ventral tray, two 20 mm upward firing cannon in the rear fuselage and one 13 mm machine-gun in the rear of the cockpit.

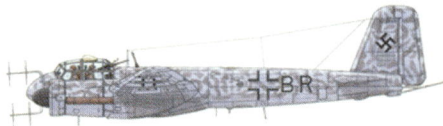

DEADLY MISSION

Loading up a Halifax. (DND PL 19507)

The Lancaster in flight. (PAC PA145613)

CANADIAN AIRMEN OVER NUREMBERG

Another airborne jamming device, *Airborne Cigar (ABC)*, was also used in conjunction with transmissions of false instructions broadcast by German-speaking Royal Air Force crew members. These transmissions were intended to confuse enemy night-fighter crews by interfering with the steady stream of information the German pilots received in the air. Of course to do this the Allies had to know the frequency bands on which the Germans were communicating. Not surprisingly the Luftwaffe constantly varied frequencies.

Serrate was a radar device designed to provide bearings on Luftwaffe fighter radar transmissions. Mosquitoes equipped with Serrate were deployed in the vicinity of known enemy beacons or airfields. The Mosquitos would then attack German fighters as they left the airfields or collected near the beacons.

However the presence of large numbers of bombers made differentiation between friend and foe extremely difficult. Consequently, and unfortunately for the Bomber Command force, *ABC* and the *Serrate* Mosquitoes achieved very little success on the night of March 30th/31st, 1944.

Other technical aids designed to increase the bombers' chances in their confrontations with enemy fighters that came on stream in 1943 and early 1944 were even less successful. *Boozer* was a passive device developed to pick up aerial transmissions from German fighters as well as those emitted by ground stations. It depended upon a system of lights that confirmed detection by the enemy. A yellow lamp signified the presence of enemy fighters; a red lamp confirmed detection by ground installations. As it turned out, enemy transmissions over its territory were so numerous that the lights remained on permanently, distracting and unsettling the bomber crews. Most switched off Boozer, relying instead upon vigilance, experience and luck for survival.

Monica was an active warning system installed at the rear of Halifax and Lancaster aircraft. It depended upon aural returns to indicate the presence of aircraft astern. Unfortunately *Monica* was unable to differentiate between friendly and hostile aircraft and the continuous clicking over the earphones proved to be an irritant rather than a help. The Monica responses were therefore ignored, or more usually, the device was switched off. A fourth technical device, Fishpond, was in effect a second H2S mounted horizontally at the rear of the aircraft. It showed aircraft in the bomber's immediate vicinity as spots or blips of light on the cathode ray screen. Those which maintained their position relative to that of the bomber were deemed to be other bombers. Any blips that converged upon the bomber were considered to be hostile interceptors. Like *Boozer* and *Monica*, difficulties of differentiation between friend and foe made Fishpond less than effective as a defensive aid.

DEADLY MISSION

Evasive Tactics

In addition to the radar assistance, survival depended on the crew's senses, operational experience, and the *corkscrew* manoeuvre. The corkscrew, although a fairly effective tactic under normal circumstances, was less effective because the heavy loads carried by Halifaxes and Lancasters considerably inhibited their manoeuverability. On receiving a gunner's warning of an impending attack the *corkscrew* required the pilot to turn sharply and simultaneously dive towards the approaching fighter, then quickly reverse direction while pulling up his aircraft into a steep climb. It was a violent manoeuvre that often scattered the navigator's dividers, pencils and protractors, and sometimes brought crew members other than the pilot to the point of nausea. Nevertheless, sound judgement and accurate directions from the gunners, together with quick reactions by the pilot, were the "sine qua non" of the *corkscrew*. Repeating the manoeuvre for as long as necessary in order to evade the attacker, while giving the gunners opportunities to shoot it down was however, physically demanding. In daylight the *corkscrew* was largely ineffective against nimbler single-engine fighters; but under cover of darkness it enabled the bomber to contend with a fair degree of success. Some crews resorted to the *corkscrew* throughout their time over enemy territory; others only when attacked. One crew from 514 Squadron reported corkscrewing for an hour during the Nuremberg raid in order to hold off fighter attacks. A Luftwaffe pilot reported the same night that he failed to complete an attack against a Lancaster because it successfully resorted to the defensive manoeuver for 45 minutes!

"Spoofs"

Another tactic meant to fool the German night-fighters was the "spoof" or diversionary attack. When a raid was mounted a certain number of aircraft would be used on spoofs. Each spoof would be intended to divert the German fighters away from the Bomber Stream.

The Route

The route the Bomber Stream would take was also predetermined and designed to try and fool the Germans. It was rarely straight and usually included several dog's legs. The route to the target was usually the most dangerous as the bombers were fully loaded and slow. The courses attempted to avoid German anti-aircraft (Flak) positions along the coast, or near major centres. To be avoided at all costs were the Luftwaffe's fighter beacons, the collection point for that region's night fighter forces.

The German Defences

By the spring of 1944 the German defences protecting their industrial heartland were quite efficient. Along the coast and around the cities the Germans had a sophisticated system of anti-aircraft guns and searchlights. In fact they had an estimated 20,625 flak guns and 6,680 searchlights deployed. Germany had taken a pounding but they were fighting back. The strength of the defences was its communications, intelligence and electronic monitoring of signals, and how that information got into the hands of their pilots.

As in the British experience, German radar played a significant role against the Allied bomber offensive. Foremost in the system were the early warning *Freya* units which were capable of detecting aircraft movements in Britain. This system could pick up the H2S waves as soon as the bombers in started up. This information was then passed to the fighter control rooms and the game of finding the Bomber Stream would start. The level of activity could tell whether what they found was the real thing or a "spoof". The German fighters would take to the air, constantly being in touch with the control room. In fact it was this system the ABC Cigar was intended to disrupt. The night-fighters would collect near the beacon closest to the anticipated path of the bombers. Then the fight would begin.

Numerous static and mobile *Würzburg* variants provided airborne fighters with information to intercept the Stream. It also controlled flak installations as well as directing the blue beam master searchlights dreaded by all Allied aircrew. The combination constituted a formidable defensive organization ranged across occupied Europe and the German heartland. By the time of the Nuremberg raid German scientists too had developed efficient airborne interception radar units, *Lichtenstein, Flensberg,* the *SN-2* and *Naxos*, which enabled Luftwaffe night fighters to detect H2S emissions from Bomber Command aircraft up to a range of 50 km. This also assisted the enemy in closing in for deadly interceptions.

German Fighter Tactics

Tame Boar

By the spring of 1944 the Reich Air Defence developed what became known as the *Zhame Sau* or *Tame Boar* system, which emphasized pursuit within the bomber stream. During a typical *Tame Boar* sortie the night fighters, usually the Messerschmitt 110 or the Junkers 88, would take-off and fly to a given radio beacon (given such names as *IDA* or *OTTO*) using a homing device for navigation. Once in position they flew a holding pattern until the ground controller identified the position of the bomber stream. Then the fighters were infiltrated into the bomber stream (often 100 km long) where interference from electronic counter-measures such as Window was less pronounced and detection by the bombers difficult. Once close they used their short-range radar to locate and close in upon their prey.

ABC Cigar was often used to try and decoy or confuse the Tame Boar pilots.

Wild Boar

In addition to facing the Luftwaffe's *Tame Boar* night-fighters swimming in the Bomber Stream, Bomber Command aircraft also had to contend with attacks from faster, more manoeverable single-engined fighters. These fighters were not equipped for night fighting, but could be utilized under specific circumstances. For the most part the Messerschmitt Bf 109's and Focke-Wulf 190's operated over or near targets in order to take advantage of the illumination afforded by flares, searchlights and fires started by the incendiaries and high explosives dropped by the attackers. Together with reflections from cloud cover, the searchlights and ground fires silhouetted the bombers enabling the nimbler fighters to swoop in from above in traditional attack fashion. They had to be very careful not to be hit by their own anti-aircraft guns, so they usually operated at altitudes of 30,000 feet or more, well above the bombers.

Code named *Wilde Sau* (Wild Boar), the single-engined attackers, entered the battle when the target had been determined. Piloted by less experienced, comparatively undisciplined pilots the Wild Boar squadrons achieved relatively minor returns in relation to their losses. They were often brought down by their flak, accidents, and fuel shortages.

Over Nuremberg the weather conditions mitigated against any significant intervention on their part.

Schräge musik

By the time of the Nuremberg attack a substantial number of the Luftwaffe's twin-engined night fighters were equipped with two upward firing 20 mm cannon. Known by the code name *Schräge Musik* (Jazz Music) the arrangement consisted of the weapons mounted in the cockpit enclosure behind the pilot, at an angle (usually sixty degrees) to fire upward and forward. Upon sighting and visually identifying his quarry silhouetted against the night sky the fighter pilot positioned himself slightly behind and a hundred to three hundred feet below the enemy aircraft. Since the Ju88s and

CANADIAN AIRMEN OVER NUREMBERG

Me110s were only slightly faster than the four-engined bomber it was comparatively easy to sidle into and maintain firing position for the brief time necessary to ensure a kill. Using a periscope gunsight the more skilled fighter pilots aimed at a point between the Halifaxes' or Lancasters' wing roots, or between the two engines. A short burst was usually enough to set them on fire, and in some cases to give a few of the seven-man bomber crews time to bail out. Since downward visibility from the Halifax and Lancaster rear turrets was almost negligible most bomber crews never realized where the attack originated and could not specify how they had been shot down.

Mother Nature's Defences

Bombing was dependent on a number of variables associated with Mother Nature, such as the season, the weather, the winds, the clouds and the moon. Because the bombing took place at night it was necessary to have the correct hours of darkness. Therefore targets deep inside Germany could only be bombed on long winter nights.

Severe weather could ground a mission. So could too much cloud or too little or the wrong type of clouds. No cloud would give enough cover for the bombers to conceal themselves from the fighters. Low cloud would obscure a target, sometimes causing an operation to be called off. Consequently the weather forecast was crucial to the success or failure of a raid.

The phases of the moon were also important as the high moon was considered too bright, and would give the night-fighters an advantage. All these items would have to be taken into consideration as to whether a raid was a "go" or was "scrubbed".

Ready for an Ops. A Halifax crew walks to their bomber.

The Nuremberg Raid, March 30th/31st 1944

"It was my last raid of the war. It was the most terrifying of all... Never before had we been sent off in moonlight... I could feel myself getting panicky, a strange feeling creeping in despite the fact we were not under attack... My gawd, if the German fighters are up tonight, we've had it."
J. Douglas Harvey, Pilot, Royal Canadian Air Force.

On the morning of March 30th, 1944, Air Chief Marshall Harris, the hard-driving Commander of Bomber Command, pondered over the daily documents. Of particular importance was the weather report which indicated a heavy, low cloud cover over northern Germany, but showed the skies to the south to be good, with only a little high cloud. Harris knew it was also late in the season for bombing raids deep into Germany, as the nights were getting shorter. The moon was also high, not a good sign for a raid.

In the last year Harris had sent his "Boys" on numerous missions against the industrial heartland of the Ruhr Valley. He had successfully devastated the City of Hamburg in the summer of 1943, but the Germans had caught up to some of his innovations and his most recent raids against Berlin had been costly.

Looking over the map he decided to attack Nuremberg. His staff did not like the conditions but could not sway Harris. Perhaps the weather was not the best, but the high clouds would counter-act the bright moon, and the raid was a "GO". The operation was code-named "Grayling".

The Target

The principal target that night was the Bavarian city of Nuremberg located deep in the heart of Adolf Hitler's Third Reich. With an estimated population of 426,000 and, according to British intelligence assessments, a potential workforce of 200,000 manning 50 major factories, 46 other commercial plants and communications facilities, 28 military and 16 Nazi Party establishments, the city constituted a target of major industrial and political importance. Moreover, Nuremberg hadn't been attacked for seven months.

The Raid is On

In the pre-briefing rooms on every base Bomber Command aircrew were briefed on the night's objectives (often without finding the name of the city until late in the afternoon). Around the airfields everyone was always conscious of the perils and problems inherent in every operation. The majority came to the pre-flight briefings with feelings of apprehension and curiosity. Once it became known that an operation was scheduled an atmosphere of suspense manifested itself on each station. On the basis of rumour and information gleaned from the Women's Auxiliary Air Force (WAAF) fuel bowser drivers, speculation about the impending trip ran riot. A light bomb load and a heavy fuel load confirmed a long flight. Speculation about the length of the flight and possible targets heightened tensions and impinged upon the moods of crews as they assembled for the pre-flight briefings, which usually took place in the late afternoon. The crews would congregate, smoking and nervously anticipating the drawing of the drapes concealing large maps of Europe on which that night's operation was plotted. Invariably, when that moment came and the Wing Commander or principal briefing officer said: "the target for tonight is...", a gasp followed by a wave of exclamations and comment swept through the room. It quickly subsided as each briefing officer detailed the operation's specifics: aiming point, navigation, weather, markers, signals, emergency facilities, intelligence, known defences, and any other aspects considered to be relevant. The details were important, but uppermost in the minds of the aircrews assembled that evening was "Will our crew be one of the lucky ones?"; "Is this it?"; "Will I see the wife again?". It would always be same theme " Will I live or die?".

Of the experienced crews sitting there when the target was announced many were speechless, some even gasped. They knew the moon conditions. They knew the clouds may not protect them. They knew it was a bad call but when they saw the route...

The Ops

Although every Bomber Command crew experienced pre-operation tensions, fears tended to subside once they became airborne. Their respective flight duties, together with the particular esprit de corps which characterized each crew took effect and exercised a calming influence. Some tended to chatter over the intercom; others resorted to a professional silence punctuated only by information or comment as required by their responsibilities. Pilots concentrated on accurate flying; navigators determined courses, positions, and calculated wind velocities; bomb aimers concerned themselves with map- reading when visibility permitted or operating the H2S; wireless operators listened for messages from or sent signals to base; engineers monitored engine performance, fuel consumption, and the aircraft's general status; gunners strained for any sign of aircraft, friendly or otherwise. Despite the relatively great numbers of aircraft involved in most Bomber Command operations, collisions were astonishingly few. Early detection and identification of an enemy aircraft was vital for survival. Then, cooperation between pilot and gunners to initiate the corkscrew or evade detection by the enemy fighter became paramount.

Other than the navigator, wireless operator, and the bomb aimer when he was operating the H2S, the rest of the crew kept an anxious watch for flak, flares, searchlight activity, and any unusual sightings that might affect the operation. On balance, flak, often a spectacular sight, didn't greatly worry most crews until they reached the target area. Then the accuracy and intensity of the anti-aircraft fire caused real concern and anxiety. Illumination of an aircraft, particularly by a radar-controlled blue beam searchlight, signified devastatingly accurate ground-fire, and was dreaded by all Bomber Command crews. Then, the most effective escape method was a steep high speed dive and tight evasive turns in order to evade the beam. Otherwise, once the bombing run was initiated it was the pilot's job to fly the aircraft according to the bomb aimer's commands until the moment of release. It was those brief critical moments - at best only a few minutes - that were extremely tense and nerve-wracking. For the gunners scanning the night sky in the face of weaving searchlights, fires and explosions below, flares, markers and flak bursts, the target area made their task especially difficult.

Once the bomb aimer"s "bombs gone", crackled over the intercom, coupled with the aircraft's tendency to balloon when its load was released, tensions eased and crew members resumed their tasks for the return flight to base. Nevertheless, a successful attack did not mean the end of danger. Junkers and Messerschmitts still prowled the bomber stream, while difficult weather, unexpected ground defences, aircraft damage or technical problems were ever present hazards during the return journey. Only when the engines were shut down at the dispersal was the operation truly over. Then, tensions eased, and cigarettes were lit. Debriefing and the post operation bacon and egg followed, confirming survival for at least another day.

The Route

Routing for the Nuremberg operation was of paramount significance. According to the plan determined for the attack the bomber force was to converge at a mid-point over the North Sea, cross the enemy coast near the Belgian city of Bruges to its first turning point over Charleroi, where it turned due east and continued on that path for 425 km. After flying for approxi-

Bomber Stream of Lancasters. (DND PL 14428)

Bombers over a target, 1945. (PAC PA202793)

DEADLY MISSION

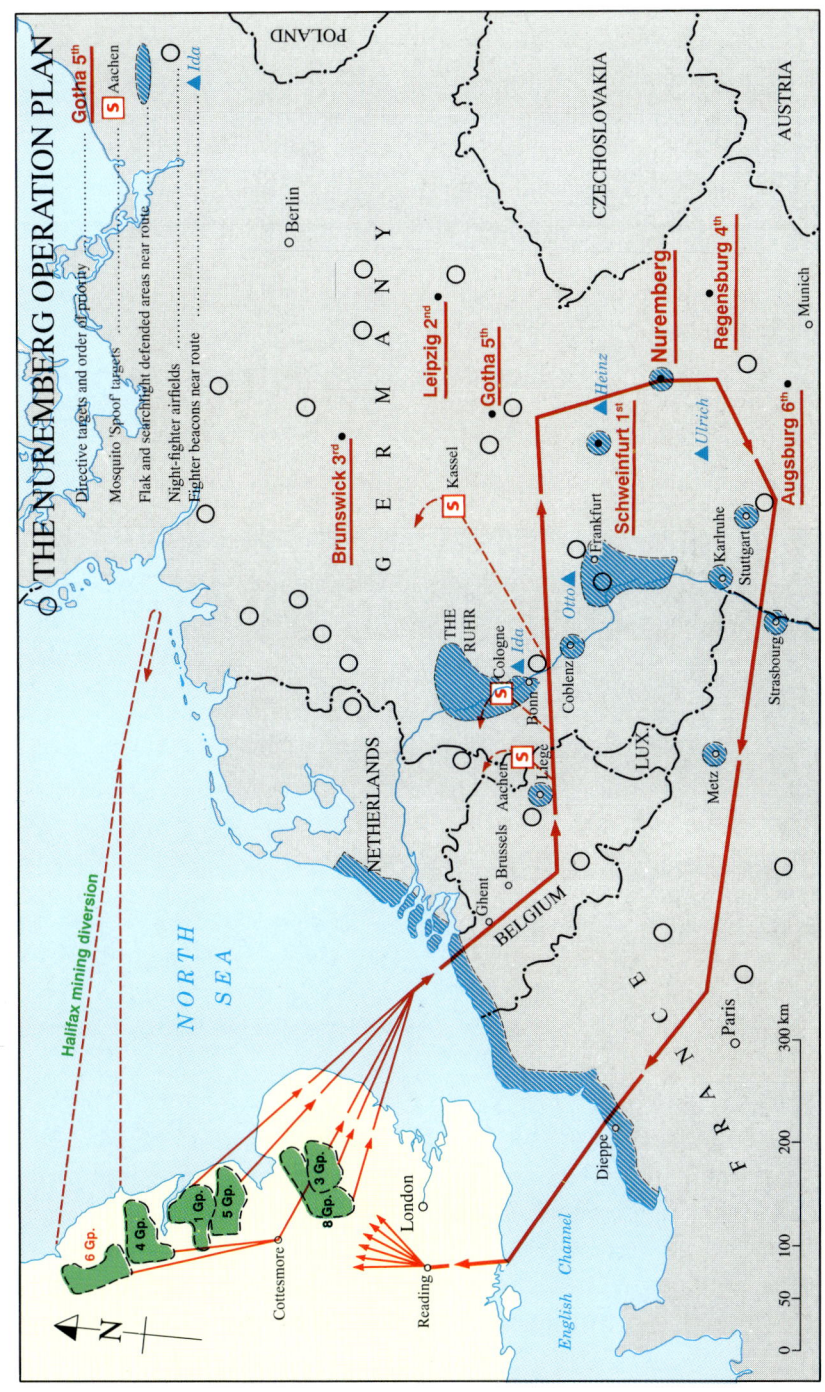

mately one hour, the Bomber Stream proceeded to the vicinity of the small German town of Fulda where it turned south for the final 126 km run to the target, now only 20 minutes away. Once over Nuremberg the bombers would drop their loads totaling 2,300 tonnes, a process taking 17 minutes. For the run home the bomber stream was briefed to follow a roundabout return track which brought it near Stuttgart and Strasbourg. The much lighter and faster bombers would then turn onto a line running northeast of Paris to the coastal town of Dieppe and finally to the south coast of England. There the force flew north where squadrons from each Group proceeded to their bases.

For the most northerly squadrons from Six Group, the Canadian Group based in the county of Yorkshire, the strike against Nuremberg meant a flight of roughly eight hours covering almost 2,560 km. For Three Group, the most southerly in Bomber Command, the flight was an hour shorter, covering a distance of some 2,100 km.

While the distances were considerable, and the weather forecast questionable, the route selected by Sir Arthur Harris aroused controversy amongst Bomber Command's Group commanders during their customary pre-operation telephone conference. In particular the long leg from Charleroi to Fulda caused concern, for it brought the bomber stream near two known German fighter beacons, IDA and OTTO, in the Bonn and Frankfurt areas, as well as the numerous airfields in their vicinities. In addition, another beacon, HEINZ, lay close to the route into the target. Nevertheless, despite objections over the choice of route from his Air Vice-Marshals, Harris, despite the meteorological uncertainties (for the choice was his and his alone), confirmed his decision to proceed with the attack that night. (To make matters worse the Germans knew the clouds in the north would prevent an attack there, so they could focus their resources in the south.)

For the aircrew there was always the possibility the weather could worsen and the raid be cancelled. This form of reprieve could occur right up to the last minute.

The Plan

On the night of March 30th-31st, 1944, 6,493 airmen, including roughly 1,500 Canadians from Six Group squadrons and those serving with Royal Air Force (RAF) units, manning 1,001 assorted aircraft, would take to the skies from airfields throughout England to attack German-held territories. The majority of the aircraft, which included 570 Lancasters, 274 Halifaxes, 117 Mosquitoes, 20 Short Stirlings, 10 Fairey Albemarles, eight Wellingtons, and six B17 Flying Fortresses, were provided by RAF Bomber Command. The

A High School Yearbook, 1944. Every school across Canada lost many students during the war. These pages come from West Hill High School, Montreal. By 1944, 55 West Hill students had died on active service.

The Story of Halifax LV 923

The history of the Nuremberg Raid is really a compilation of the individual stories of a thousand aircrews. For some the night passed uneventfully, for others it was a terrifying mission, and for some it was their last night on earth.

One of the 900 bombers that took part in the raid was Halifax LV 923, 427 (Lion) Squadron, of the Number 6 (RCAF) Bomber Group.

The crew was skippered by George Laird of Winnipeg, Navigator was George Lorimer, Bomb/Aimer, Joe Corbally, Mid-Upper Gunner was Jim Moffat of Timmins, Flight Engineer was Bill Cardy, Wireless Operator was Pat Clapham of Ireland and the Rear Gunner was Jack Findley. Since September 1943 they had participated in missions to Hanover, Mannheim, Kassel, Dusseldorf, Leipzig, twice to Berlin, thrice to Frankfort and once to Le Mans. By March 1944 they were an experienced crew. Their next Ops was to be the 13th for some of them. The crew now consisted of Laird, Corbally, Clapham, Moffat (now Rear Gunner), and Lloyd Smith, Mid-Upper Gunner, "Red" Soeder, Navigator and Jock Morrison of the Royal Air Force, Flight Engineer.

Crew at RCAF Station Leeming, England 1943. Left to right, back row: Sgt. Pat Clapham wag RAF, Sq/Ldr George Laird DFC pilot, W01 Joe Corbally b/a, F/O Paddy McClune f/e RAF. *Seated front:* Sgt Lloyd Smith, Sgt George Lorimer nav.

DEADLY MISSION

aerial armada even included four United States Army Air Force (USAAF) fighters. Code-named Grayling this mission became what has been described as the greatest single air battle of the Second World War.

Of the aerial armada, 162 were designated to carry out "spoofs", diversionary and bomber support roles. Mosquitoes from number Eight Group Pathfinder Force were to make spoof raids on three German cities; Aachen, Cologne and Kassel. Mosquitoes from 100 Group flew anti-night-fighter sorties with the bomber stream. Fifty Halifaxes from Four and Six Groups, were to act as a diversionary force, timing their approach to the German coast to coincide with the moment the main strike force reached the Belgian shore 320 km to the south. Twenty Stirlings, 10 Albemarles, eight Wellingtons and six Fortresses would occupy themselves with agent and supply drops to Resistance groups, mining operations in Dutch and French waters, leaflet distribution, and monitoring and disrupting Luftwaffe radio traffic.

The Main Force

According to the plan the operation was due to begin at 21:15 (9:15 pm), with the first aircraft taking off from the most northerly stations in Yorkshire. Pathfinder, Mosquitoes and Lancasters, together with their main force counterparts followed, forming a stream of aircraft divided into five sections distributed between 17,000 and 23,000 feet. The first aircraft were scheduled to be over the target at 1:00 am on March 31st. Nine Pathfinder Mosquitoes were to drop Window to distract the radar-predicted anti-aircraft ground defences. They were to be followed five minutes later by 24 Pathfinder Lancasters dropping flares and Target Indicators to mark the aiming point, a warehouse near the main railway station. Next, at 1:07 am according to the planned timetable, six more Lancasters were designated to verify the aiming point visually and if necessary, correct any error in the initial placement of the Target Indicators. Three minutes later the first wave of the main force was to begin its attack, with bombing planned to end at 1:22 am. This was the theoretical plan as drawn up by Bomber Command's headquarters on the morning and afternoon of March 30th, 1944. But theory and practice, as the Nuremberg raid confirmed, rarely coincide.

Across the airfields the crews anxiously awaited the decision to Stand Down, but it never came. Aware of the difficult task ahead they also knew the survival rates were bad at the best of times. For every 100 aircrew completing a tour of Operations 51 would die in action and 9 in accidents. Only 24 would survive unscathed. Today it is hard to imagine the effects of such statistics on the brave young men awaiting their fate on those English runways

Bombs Away by Paul Goranson (CWM 11327)

DEADLY MISSION

and it is hard to gauge the amount of courage required to board the aircraft, and fly into those darkened skies.

"... you checked your watch again and again, waiting for the time to dress... The sudden mingling of the crew brought some life to the squadron and the corny jokes and one liners got more than their deserved share of laughter... 'Does your mother know you're flying tonight?'... 'Anyone want to leave their girlfriend's phone number with me?'... 'I got a new parachute today and they told me to bring it back if it doesn't work.' Old tired jokes."
J. Douglas Harvey, Pilot, Royal Canadian Air Force.

"...I noticed the whole crew were nervous. Four of them had already started eating their flying rations and the young Flight Engineer kept taking his helmet off and putting it back on again. His face was covered in perspiration. I have no doubt at all that they had a premonition that they were for the chop that night."
E.M. Butler, Leading Aircraftwoman, Woman's Auxiliary Air Force.
The aircraft was shot down by a German night-fighter on the Long Leg. There were no survivors. The pilot was J.H. Thornton of Dundas, Ontario.

The Mission

Gradually one by one the bombers took off, in all 795 Lancasters and Halifaxes headed towards Nuremberg. For a lucky few mechanical problems forced them to return to base, but for the others there could be no such luck.

Ominously, the Zephyr reporting system broke down during the Nuremberg raid; and unexpectedly stronger winds, particularly on the long leg, caused the bomber stream to stray from the assigned track and delayed its reaching the target on time. Together with increased cloud cover over Nuremberg and late and inaccurate marking by the Pathfinders, the attack would become scattered and sporadic instead of concentrated and intensive.

The Bomber Stream, more than 100 km in length, collected over the North Sea. Over the Belgian coast the predicted cloud cover dissipated and, unexpectedly and very unusual for the normal operational heights at which Bomber Command operated, condensation caused by the bomber's exhaust emissions left a very visible trail across the moonlit sky. The wind velocity predicted by the Command meteorologist proved to be misleading. Instead of providing an expected 60-80 km per hour tail wind during the outward-bound portion of the route, the wind speed increased and changed direction. Together with the failure of the windfinders to provide a sufficient number of returns to enable Bomber Command headquarters to average their findings, the true wind velocity caused the bomber stream to scatter northwards, bring-

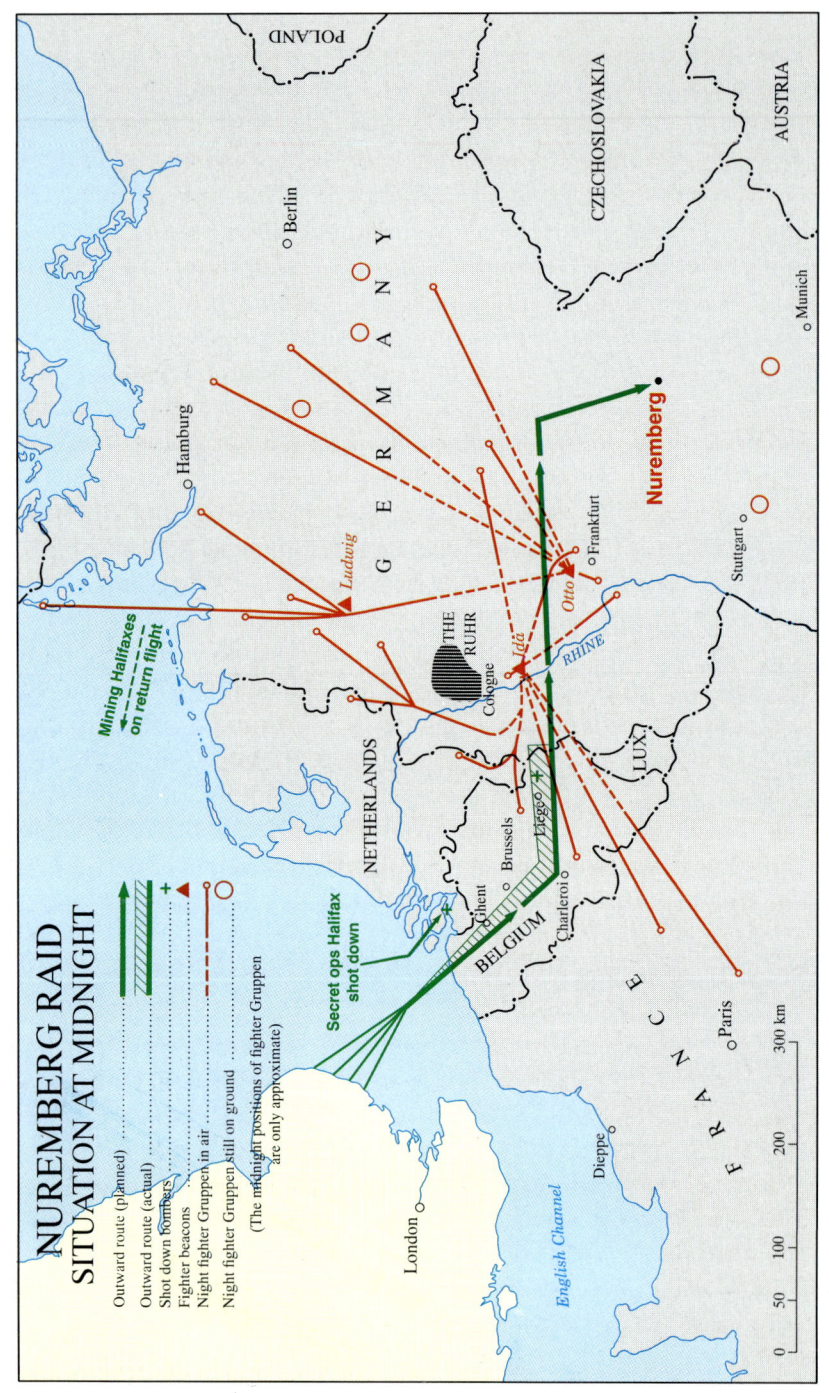

ing it nearer to the Luftwaffe's fighter beacons, airfields and anti-aircraft installations. Subsequently failure to find and apply accurate wind velocities led to inaccurate-timed runs and target marking errors. Thus, particularly throughout the long leg from Charleroi to Fulda, the combination of moonlight, lack of cloud cover, condensation trails at height, scattering of the bomber stream, and unexpectedly poor visibility over the target area, favoured the Luftwaffe defences. Together with the Luftwaffe's early and correct surmise that Nuremberg was that night's primary objective, the German fighter and anti-aircraft defences were able to effectively locate and move against the Bomber Command attack.

From the Nuremberg raid's early moments meteorological conditions favoured the defenders. Knowing that the weather conditions in the north of Germany were unfavourable for major operations in that area, the Reich Air Defence controllers concentrated upon determining the probable target. Soon after the bomber force turned on to the long undeviating leg to Fulda and particularly after the unexpectedly high winds caused it to pass almost directly over the fighter beacon *IDA*, the defenders correctly deduced that Nuremberg was the likely target. That determination in turn enabled the Luftwaffe's night-fighter force to concentrate its available serviceable resources, 361 twin-engined types and 150 single-engined aircraft, against the bomber stream in what became a triumph of pursuit. The hunt was on.

Luftwaffe aircraft quickly located the Bomber Stream and fired flares to help guide the Junkers and Messerschmitts towards the attacking force. Despite deployment of Window their very numbers enabled the German ground radars to track the stream with ease. It was the Tame Boar twin-engined Ju88s and Me110s infiltrating into the bomber stream that inflicted many casualties upon the attacking force. Although little faster than the Bomber Command Halifaxes and Lancasters the German aircraft were formidable adversaries.

The night-fighters slipped into position within the bomber stream. SN-2 equipped German aircraft, unaffected by Window, could pick up a British bomber at a distance of roughly 6km. This enabled them with their superior speed, to home in upon the quarry. Aircraft not equipped with the most advanced airborne interception electronics used the moonlight conditions to greatly facilitate their efforts to close with their adversaries. For those armed with *Schräge Musik* success came easily.

Frustration and fear co-mingled during the Nuremberg raid. For the German pursuers frustration surfaced when they were unable to close quickly upon their victims; for the Mosquitoes riding herd on the bomber stream the problem was one of identification. Since the Ju88s and Me110s were only

The Story of Hailfax LV 923; continued

On March 30th, 1944 the men knew that the phase of the moon would likely mean all Ops would be cancelled. To their surprise the men were told to "Hang around", that a mission was "On". They speculated on what it would be and concluded "a nice French target", because Germany was out of the question. But their pleasure quickly soured when they noticed extra fuel tanks being loaded onto the Halifax. It was a bad Omen.

In the late afternoon the crews of both 427 and 429 Squadrons, about 140 men, met in the Briefing Room. They sat nervously as the Commanding Officer pulled back the curtain covering a large map of Europe. It revealed the night's target was Nuremberg. There was a gasp in the room, as the thoughts of a long trip in the bright moonlight flashed premonitions of disaster. The crew of LV 923 was no different. "We'll be dead ducks in the bright moonlight" and "the fighters won't even have to search" for us, were their thoughts.

Breaking from the briefing the men went to their aircraft. There was "not a good feel to this at all", and the general view was that "We're in for it". Some of the men rested. At 8 pm they went for dinner, the usual pre-Ops meal of bacon and poached eggs. Laird was typically nervous before a raid and tonight was no different. He graciously gave his egg to the Rear Gunner, Jim Moffat. There was no conversation over the meal. Later they received a briefing from the Meteorological Officer, then a chat on German defences, and an explanation of the target.

For the Ops Halifax LV923 was going to have a "Second Dickey", a rookie pilot or "sprog", along to gain experience. Arthur Stainton of Peterborough was the 8th man on the crew. They got their parachutes, put on their flying gear and went out to the aircraft. The pilot and navigator prepared the course, the four Hercules engines roared into action and they waited for their turn to take-off. One-by-one the aircraft of 427 and 429 Squadrons lifted off and the mission to Nuremberg was underway.

Each aircraft had a special position in the Bomber Stream, and all over England "groups of aircraft all over the sky" would appear and "all of a sudden, they'd turn at a certain time, like a flock of birds heading south, and after half an hour you'd see nothing". The aircraft would be hidden in the night.

marginally faster than the four-engined heavies, pursuit was generally prolonged and often inconclusive. That drawback however, was offset by the opportunities afforded by the great number of potential victims, and the element of surprise which had been greatly enhanced by the introduction of *Schräge Musik*. Most of the crews lost were unaware of their attackers until it was too late to take evasive action. Using *Schräge Musik* during the Nuremberg raid Oberleutnant Martin Becker scored seven confirmed kills: two PFF Lancasters and one Main Force Lancaster and four Halifaxes, a record for a single night's operation that was exceeded only once in December 1943.

The experiences of those who returned reported dramatic, extraordinary actions and escapes from damaged aircraft. Fire was the great fear for Bomber Command crews, and neither the Halifax nor the Lancaster enjoyed any advantage in that regard. Both burned quickly and with equal ferocity, flashing spectacularly across the night sky like falling torches. According to crews who survived the Nuremberg operation, falling aircraft pricked the darkness as they struck the ground and exploded. In those planes were many of their friends. With so many aircraft going down at least one crew during the Nuremberg raid was ordered by its captain to stop recording numbers. Of Bomber Command's two principal heavy bombers, the Halifax, because of its crew disposition, afforded the greatest possibilities for survival. With the bomb-aimer, navigator and wireless operator located in the nose and with the escape hatch situated directly below the navigator's position, exit from a doomed Halifax was twice as likely than from the Lancaster. Such an advantage however, offered small comfort for Halifax crews. Amazingly, many men escaped from a doomed bomber and their stories of extraordinary escapes from both types of aircraft border on the unbelievable.

"I watched horrified as a twin-engined fighter flew up the white vapour trails of the bombers on my left. Lancasters were rearing up in flames, exploding into fireballs as their bomb loads blew up and they plunged over and down. Others were being hit with cannon shells, fires raced along their wings as they began the long drop through the clouds below... Tracers were criss-crossing the sky as the German fighters found their range... We like all others were sitting ducks, silhouetted against the solid cloud layer below... The crew were silent, frozen with fear... Dim shapes suddenly erupted into balls of fire as bomber after bomber blew up, their explosions lighting the sky and then slowly fading as they disintegrated."
J. Douglas Harvey, Pilot, Royal Canadian Air Force.

The high degree of visibility due to moonlight proved to be of significant advantage to the Luftwaffe night-fighters. They resorted to the standard tactic of attacking from below and behind. Known as the *von unten hinten* method, the fighter raised its nose at the *moment juste*, fired, and allowed the bomber to fly through the burst from its cannons and machine guns.

"Weather was marvelous - clear sky, half-moon, little cloud and no mist - it was simply ideal, almost too bright. It was a Lancaster flying nicely on a steady course so that, when we were comfortably positioned underneath and from about 50 metres, Drewes (the pilot) opened fire with the upward firing cannon at one wing which immediately caught fire. We followed the Lancaster for five minutes until it crashed below with a tremendous explosion."
Erich Handke, Unteroffizier, German Air Force.

"...I got an SN-2 contact at a distance of five km... we flew very carefully under the left-hand plane and fired from roughly 80 metres. The first burst hit at once and our opponent caught fire in the left wing... a few seconds later we were under the second machine... we acted quickly... It was some time before the two planes hit the ground with terrific explosions. Coloured cascades and "Christmas trees" burnt on the ground... so they were Pathfinders..."
W. Heidenbach, Oberfeldwebel, German Air Force.

"Within seconds, the bomber burst into flames, banked and lost height quickly... The bomber broke into two burning parts which soon afterwards hit the ground."
Fritz Lau, Oberleutnant, German Air Force.

For an hour the Halifaxes and Lancasters of Bomber Command ran the gauntlet of marauding Luftewaffe fighters, as well as searchlight and flak defences in the vicinities of Liege, Bonn and other points along the route. In addition to the flares dropped by the defenders to indicate the bomber stream's progress, its path was increasingly marked by the remains of doomed aircraft blazing as they fell and burned on the ground.

All along the long leg the bombers were falling. Aircrew could see in the darkness the fire of an aircraft in trouble or the explosion of a fully-loaded bomber. The swarm of enemy fighters was devastating the Stream. The more the wind and the evasive action spread out the bombers the easier was the task of the German pilots. They had not even reached the Fulda turning point.

DEADLY MISSION

Driven over the IDA fighter beacon by the unpredicted winds, and flying in brilliant, cloudless moonlight conditions, which illuminated the long streams of condensation trails left by the bombers, the conditions proved to be fatal. Despite the methods employed by the bombers, the corkscrew and the efforts of the air-gunners along 425 km track between the turning point over Charleroi and Fulda, 59 Halifaxes and Lancasters were lost. The long leg claimed 41 Lancasters and 18 Halifaxes, perhaps the greatest number of casualties incurred in the shortest time in the history of aerial combat.

By the time the Bomber Stream veered south for the 20 minute run to the target, many had been delayed, were off-course or damaged. A further dozen had gone down. Over the flame-lit target the crews quickly dropped their bombs, but the anti-aircraft flak was heavy and the aircraft were rocked by the explosions. Occasionally a direct hit would cause a bomber to explode or if a wing was shot off the bomber would start a slow spinning descent into the flaming city below. Here there were further losses as Wild Boar fighters swooped down on the attackers The moonlight favoured the *Wilde Sau* defenders, but despite the highly favourable flying conditions they fortunately had little success. Searchlights cut the darkness and should a bomber be coned by several of the searchlight beams, the brightness would blind the pilot and the flak would concentrate its fire. A further ten bombers were lost near or over Nuremberg.

None-the-less, more than 700 bombers made it through and dropped their load. They had little to contemplate their accuracy. A number dropped on locations close to it or on secondary targets.

After bombing they turned to make the run home. They still had to fly more than 600 km across Germany or German-occupied France. Over Stuttgart three more planes went down. Many planes that were damaged or had lost their navigational aids struggled to make their way back. If a nightfighter caught them in this condition they were done for. But one advantage they did have was that flying empty they were as fast as the Germans.

Gradually they limped home and at all the airfields ground crew waited for the "Boys" to come home and to take account of the night's terrific losses. Nine crippled bombers crashed in England. They had almost made it. After they landed the crews would be de-briefed and an analysis of the Mission made. By 7:25 am the Nuremberg Raid was over.

"Our crews did what we always did at these times. We got drunk."
F.J. Parker, Flying Officer, Royal Air Force.

The Story of Halifax LV 923; continued

Early in the flight LV 923 ran into problems when their H2S radar broke down. With the radar out, the navigator, "Red" Soeder had to manually calculate the route, but the winds were much stronger than they were told and keeping on course was going to be a problem. In 20 minutes they were over Belgium, turning onto the Long Leg to Germany," flying between two layers of cloud, a heavy, thick cloud well below and a thin thin layer above us, and the moon was coming down through it." The bombers were "like flies crawling across a lit ceiling".

The Rear Gunner, Jim Moffat, was responsible for reporting aircraft to the pilot and within 30 minutes on the Long Leg he reported seeing 22 aircraft going down in flames, a mile to the left of LV 923. "I saw aircraft go down", like seeing "a little flaming beetle, a mile or two away". He could not "see the plane, just the flames and a bit of the aircraft when it started plunging". Moffat "had never seen anything like it before". Finally Laird told Jim "That's enough. Tell me no more". Without the radar Soeder had to estimate the turn that would bring them over the target, and the best he could offer was "I think we should turn now". Stainton saw the glow of a city on fire, and the Halifax banked to make the final run. Finally they reached Nuremberg, they were "at 20,000 feet, just above the clouds, big rolling clouds below us, with the glow of the city underneath". They saw no marker flares designating the target and only one other bomber over the city. They saw "a German fighter coming straight at the other bomber. They collided and the collision "cut the tail right off the bomber" and the "bomber started to spin flat like a leaf" as it fell into the burning city. LV 923 dropped their bomb load over the city centre and the crew all heard "We're going home".

Without the radar and being affected by the strong winds the Halifax was quickly off course. Soeder signaled "I'm sorry Skipper, we're way off course". As they turned to regain the correct route home, they heard Laird scream over the intercom "What the Hell!" Out of nowhere a Lancaster of 622 Squadron, also off course, brushed over the top of LV 923, cutting through the fuselage, its propellers cutting like a saw. The impact knocked off the tail fin of LV 923, and the aircraft was doomed. Slowly, like the bomber over Nuremberg, it began a flat spin to earth.

Later in England LV 923 was reported "DID NOT RETURN", and the eight man crew, listed as "MISSING". They were among the many casualties of the deadly mission over Nuremberg.

No. 427 Squadron, R.C.A.F.

April, 22nd., 1944.

Dear Mrs. Moffat :

    Before receiving this letter you will have had a telegram informing you that your son, Flying Officer James Moffat of this Squadron has been reported missing as the result of Air Operations on the 30th/31st., of March, 1944.

    It is with the deepest regret that I write to you this date to convey to you the deep feelings of my entire Squadron. On the night of March 30th., Jim and his fellow Crew members took off from this aerodrome to carry out a Night Bombing Attack on Germany and were due to return the following morning. Unfortunately, the aircraft never returned and we have had no communication from it, nor from any member of the Crew since time of take-off.

    We lost one of our best Crews when this aircraft did not return from this Operation and we count it's loss a bitter blow to the strength of this Squadron.

    Jim was popular with all ranks of this Squadron's personnel and active in all Station activities. He had already completed a total of ten Operational trips with this Squadron over enemy territory and was considered to be one of our best Gunners. At all times he carried out his duties as an Officer and a gentleman in a most exemplary manner. We shall miss him greatly.

    There is always the possibility of course that Jim may be a prisoner-of-war, in which case you will either hear from him direct or through the Air Ministry who will in turn receive advice from the International Red Cross Society.

    Your son's effects have been gathered together and forwarded to the Royal Air Force Central Depository where they will be held until better news is received, or in any event for a period of at least six months before being despatched to you through the Administrator of Estates, Ottawa.

    May I now express to you the deep and heartfelt sympathy of my entire Squadron in your grievous anxiety, - an anxiety in which we all share. I would like to assure you also how greatly we all honour the heroic sacrifice your son has made for the Cause of Freedom, so far from home in the Service of the British Commonwealth of Nations.

Mrs. Elizabeth L. Moffat,
Drawer II,
Castleton,
Ontario, Canada.

(R.S. Turnbull) Wing Commander,
Officer Commanding,
No. 427 Squadron, R.C.A.F.

Nuremberg - The Analysis

About dawn on March 31st, 1944 the grim list of downed and missing aircraft was compiled and the cost of the Nuremberg Raid calculated. A total of 95 bombers were missing and a further ten crashed in Britain. In addition, one was scrapped due to extreme battle damage. Seventy others were damaged. In Bomber Command terminology a raid that lost 5% of the attacking force was considered to be an unacceptable casualty rate. The losses over Nuremberg totalled 13.1%. The results of the bombing indicated only 11 Luftwaffe and 8 flak unit casualties, 256 buildings damaged, 60 German and 15 foreign workers killed and 100 injured, and 11,000 or so citizens displaced from their dwellings. It was hardly a success.

However the losses sustained by the aircrew far outweighed any effects on the Germans. In all 545 men died, including 112 Canadians, while 159 aircrew were made prisoners. Without doubt Sir Arthur Harris' gamble on weather and the possibility of surprising the Luftwaffe defenders by his boldness was a failure. But what went wrong?

It seems just about everything did. The diversionary operations did not fool the Germans. The navigational difficulties due to high winds en route to Nuremberg scattered the bomber stream, the cloud cover obscured the city which made visual corroboration of the aiming point extremely difficult, the late arrival of both Pathfinders and the main force, coupled with PFF's inaccurate marking, ensured that the strike failed. The high clouds that would have shielded the Bomber Stream did not materialize. The moonlight was too much of an advantage for the enemy. Nuremberg was an aberration, a culmination of everything that could go wrong going wrong.

Nuremberg was a turning point in Bomber Command's approach to its tactical use in the aerial war against Germany. After Nuremberg the Bomber Command never again committed its entire strength against a single target. It also marked the high point in the war for the German night-fighter operations.

In the wider context of the aerial assault upon Germany, the Nuremberg operation that March night in 1944 highlighted the Nazi Reich's massive defensive preparations against Bomber Command's attacks: the allocation of an estimated 15% of the Luftwaffe's total number of aircraft for the defence of the Fatherland; the deployment of almost one million men and women to operate 20,625 anti-aircraft guns and 6,800 searchlights; the production, establishment and maintenance of large stockpiles of anti-aircraft ammunition severely taxed Nazi Germany's resources. This severely strained the already stretched German armament industries. The Nazis could ill afford this loss of manpower and munitions. (It has been estimated that it took 3,343 shells fired

DEADLY MISSION

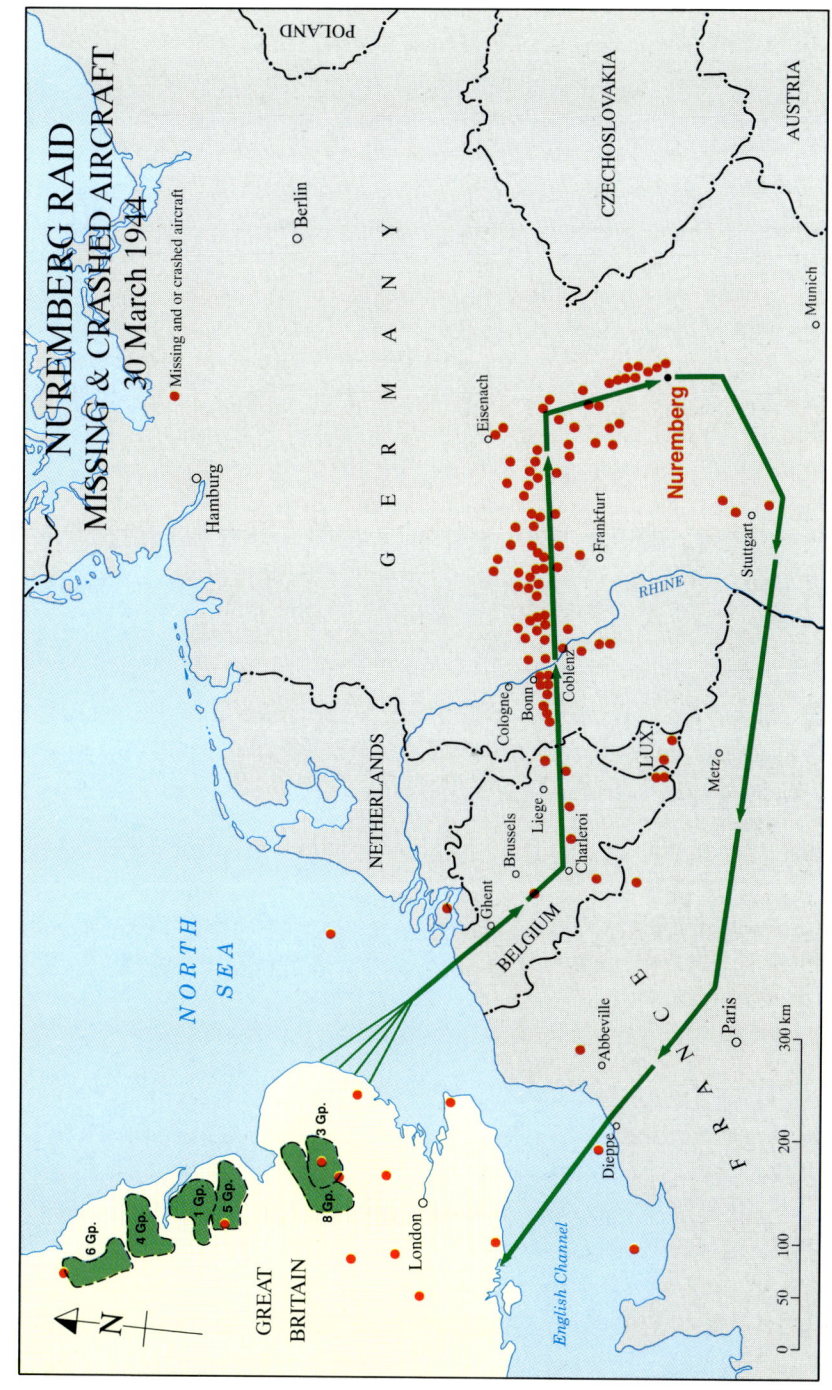

The Story of Halifax LV 923 - Epilogue

Over the next month there was no news of the men. Finally, through German sources, the bad news came in. George Laird, "Red" Soeder, Joe Corbally, Bill Clapham, Art Stainton and Lloyd Smith were reported killed. Their bodies had been found with the wreckage of LV 923. It was likely they were killed in the collision or knocked unconscious and died on impact. Jock Morrison was later reported to have died of injuries sustained when he landed in the trees. It appeared he had got out of the Halifax.

Jim Moffat was still missing, but he had survived, and had been taken in by the local resistance. He evaded capture until finally liberated by the advancing Allies six months later. Only then were the final minutes of Halifax LV 923 explained.

Jim had heard Laird yell "What the Hell!" and felt the impact of the collision. He said "it stunned me, but I thought we were O.K. because we were still flying straight. I called on the intercom but there was no answer, I unhooked myself and tried to crawl out, but the door leading to the fuselage was crushed. I thought we had tough times before, but we made it back. I looked to the left and saw no tail fin, and said to myself "Oh dear God, we're done for."

He put on his chute and crawled out of the gun turret. He stated: "I was standing on the wheel housing, out in space. I hooked the chute and pulled the chord before I jumped, but fortunately held it tight so it didn't open. I knelt on the turret and saw the top of the fuselage all torn off. I was falling at the same speed as the aircraft and was kicking at it to get away." Finally he was "yanked by the chute as it opened with a 'crack' and soon I was swinging back and forth". He thought that "the war is over for me".

Moffat woke the next morning in a field. He could hear church bells and thought to himself he "must have been really drunk last night". Looking at the parachute he saw "blood all over it" and then he realized it wasn't a dream.

Jim Moffat was the only survivor of the two aircraft that collided that night. Fourteen men had perished on the route home. Today Moffat's comrades of LV 923 rest side-by-side in Hotton War Cemetery in Belgium. Only Jock Morrison is not there. He is buried in a small churchyard on the Belgian border. To Jim Moffat, on that night March 31st, 1944, his "whole family died".

by 88mm gun batteries to bring down one Bomber Command aircraft.).

As a postscript although the Nuremberg raid caused little significant damage to the city and its production facilities it was, in essence, a harbinger of its ultimate fate. After the Allies established themselves in Europe following the successful invasion in June 1944, and once technical aids to navigation were installed on the continent, Bomber Command's attacks against targets within Germany became much more precise and effective. On January 2nd, 1945, Bomber Command once again attacked Nuremberg in force and the city experienced the destruction and harsh realities that it had escaped during the earlier raids. In some respects its fate that night was retribution for those Allied airmen who had fallen during their attack the previous spring.

In a final twist, Nuremberg, the Nazi Party's ideological home, was chosen as the site for the Great War crimes trials of Hitler's cronies. It was at Nuremberg where the great proponents of Adolf Hitler's inhumane policies were found guilty of Crimes Against Humanity, and executed.

In the end 55,573 "Boys" of Bomber Command died in the night skies, delivering the mortal blows to Hitler's tyranny. They knew that their sacrifices would not be in vain and that their courage and spirit would win the day. Nine thousand and nine hundred and nineteen were Canadian "Boys".

They shall not be forgotten.

Bibliography - Suggested Reading
The Nuremberg Raid by Martin Middlebrook. London, 1980.
Wings for Victory by Spencer Dunmore. Toronto, 1994.
Behind Enemy Lines by M. Thomas. Belleville, 2001.
Boys, Bombs and Brussels Sprouts by J. Douglas Harvey. Toronto, 1981.
The Crucible of War 1939 - 1945 by B. Greenhous, S.J. Harris. Toronto, 1994.
History of the German Night Fighter Force 1939-45 by G. Aders, London, 1979.
Pathfinder by D.C.T Bennett. London, 1983.
Soldier at Bomber Command by Charles Carrington.. London, 1989.
Bomber Offensive by Sir Arthur Harris. London, 1947.
The Bombers by N. Longmate. London, 1982.
Royal Air Force 1939 -1945. Vol. III; by H.S. Saunders. London, 1954 .
"Bomber" Harris; The Authorized Biography by D. Saward. London, 1984.
The Strategic Air Offensive Against Germany. Volumes I-IV; by Sir C. Webster and N. Frankland. London, 1961.

Canada's Roll of Honour, Nuremberg March 30th/31st, 1944
Lest We Forget

Allen, P/O Jack, Toronto, Ontario. Age 32
Anderson, W.O.Frederick, Winnipeg, Manitoba. Age 21
Anderson, F/Sgt Lloyd, Craigmyle, Alberta. Age 27
Atkins, P/O Robert, Petrolia, Ontario. Age 27 A
Awrey, P/O Donald, Windsor, Ontario. Age 23
Baker, P/O Nicholas, London, Ontario. Age 22
Beach, W.O. Roy, Winnipeg, Manitoba. Age 29
Belyea, P/O Allan, Winnipeg, Manitoba. Age 21
Berry, P/O John, Roland, Manitoba. Age 21
Bissett, S/L Jack, St Vital, Manitoba. Age 23
Bradshaw, Sgt Allan, Rockcliffe, Ontario. Age 20
Brockway, P/O George, Mimico, Ontario. Age 21
Burke, P/O David, Hamilton, Ontario. Age 25
Carey, F/L Douglas, Brandon, Manitoba. Age 22
Carleton, F/O Reginald, Kingston, Ontario. Age 22
Clark, P/O Harold, Maxville, Ontario. Age 21
Clarkson, P/O Robert, Hamilton, Ontario. Age 20
Coffey, Sgt Harry, Saint John, New Brunswick. Age 21
Corbally, P/O Joseph, Toronto, Ontario. Age 24
Cracknell, F/L Walter, Fort William, Ontario. Age 22
Craig, F/O James, Winnipeg, Manitoba. Age 22
Crosland, W.O. Alfred, Toronto, Ontario. Age 22
Cruse, F/O William, Winnipeg, Manitoba. Age 21
Cullen, P/O Sidney, Atikokan, Ontario. Age 24
De Witt, P/O Arthur, Woodstock, N.B. Age 20
Death, P/O Arthur, Toronto, Ontario. Age 23
Devoy, P/O Alexander, Cumberland, British Columbia
Digney, F/L Roderick, Edmonton, Alberta. Age 29
Dixon, F/O William, Aulac, New Brunswick. Age 21
Doig, F/O John, Winnipeg, Manitoba. Age 31
Ducharme, F/O Joseph Jean, Montreal, Quebec. Age 25
Edmonson, P/O Norman, Brantford, Ontario. Age 20
Ferguson, F/Sgt Lloyd, New Glasgow, N.S. Age 28
Ferrier, F/O James, Mimico, Ontario. Age 23
Gourdeau, F/O Arthur, Hollywood, California. Age 22
Hall, P/O William, Middleton, Nova Scotia. Age20
Hammond, F/O Douglas, Port Dover, Ontario. Age 22
Harnish, F/Sgt Clyde, Halifax, Nova Scotia. Age 24
Harris, P/O John, St Johns, Newfoundland. Age 29
Hawkes, P/O Lloyd, Leamington, Ontario. Age 20
Haycock, P/O Roy, London, Ontario. Age 25
Hergott, P/O Gerard, Waterloo, Ontario. Age 20
Jarvis, F/Sgt Everett, Quebec City, Quebec. Age 22
Johnston, W.O. Ernest, Brantford, Ontario. Age 21
Kellow, P/O Leslie, Victoria, British Columbia. Age 25
Kruger, F/O Carl, Neudorf, Saskatchewan. Age 24
Laberge, W.O. Daniel, Sudbury, Ontario. Age 22
Labow, F/O John, Beachburg, Ontario. Age 22
Laidlaw, F/O James, Tranquille, B.C. Age 20
Laird, S/L George, Winnipeg, Manitoba. Age 29
Latham, P/O Jim, Windsor, Ontario. Age 19
Lavery, F/O Thomas, Listowel, Ontario. Age 28
Leatherdale, P/O Charles, Toronto, Ontario. Age 27
LeClaire, F/O Joseph J., Outremont, Quebec. Age 22
Litchfield, F/O Ralph, Winnipeg, Manitoba. Age 27
MacAuley, F/O Norman, New Westminster, B.C.

Majchrowicz, P/O F.R., Winnipeg, Manitoba
Maw, P/O Arthur, Winnipeg, Manitoba
McCreary, P/O J.D., Windsor, Ontario
McInnes, P/O Jack, Toronto, Ontario. Age 20
McIntyre, Sgt Donald, Winnipeg, Manitoba. Age 23
McNay, F/Sgt Irvin, Toronto, Ontario. Age 29
McPhee, F/O Walter, Vancouver, B. C. Age 23
Merritt, W.O. John, North Battleford, Sask. Age 28
Metzler, S/L Harry, Fort William, Ontario. Age 30
Milward, P/O Leo, Regina, Saskatchewan.
Mitchell, F/Sgt Percy, Ottawa, Ontario. Age 24
Mogalki, W.O. Roy, Goodwater, Saskatchewan. Age 23
Mouchet, W.O. Maurice, St. Boniface, Man. Age 26
Munnery, F/O Norman, Ottawa, Ottawa. Age 22
Munro, F/O George, Vancouver, B.C. Age 25
Narum, P/O Chester, Rosemary, Alberta. Age 23
O'Brien, F/O Charles, Toronto, Ontario. Age 28
Orr, P/O Hubert, Peace River, Alberta. Age 30
Osborn, F/O Roy, Brantford, Ontario. Age25
Paquin, F/O Florent, St Boniface, Manitoba. Age 24
Pattison, Sgt Allen, Billings Bridge, Ontario. Age 23
Patton, P/O Alvin, Margaret, Manitoba. Age29
Peppiatt, P/O Franklin, Toronto. Ontario. Age 20
Preece, P/O Gordon, Vancouver, B.C. Age 19
Rathwell, P/O Robert, Billings Bridge, Ontario. Age 19
Reid, F/O Earle, Milford Station, Nova Scotia. Age 23
Rice, W.O. Alan., Toronto, Ontario. Age 20
Robinson, F/O Leroy, Golden, B.C. Age 27
Rost, W.O. William, Cornwall, Ontario. Age 22
Rush, P/O Edward, Calgary, Alberta. Age 22
Saprunoff, P/O Samuel, Trail, B.C. Age 22
Sargent, F/Sgt William, New Hazelton, B.C. Age 20
Sehlin, P/O Donald, Millet, Alberta. Age 20
Shannon, F/O Robert, Winnipeg, Manitoba. Age 21
Sheahan, P/O John, Douglas, Ontario.
Shoener, W.O. Kenneth, Belleville, Ontario. Age 22
Smith, P/O Lloyd, Sturgis, Saskatchewan. Age 24
Soeder, F/O William, Saskatoon, Saskatchewan. Age 26
Stainton, F/Sgt Arthur, Hampton, Ontario. Age 27
Taylor, F/L John, Winnipeg, Manitoba. Age 23
Thibodeau, F/Sgt Roy, Pine Falls, Manitoba. Age 23
Thomson, F/O Richard, Saskatoon, Sask. Age 23
Thornton, P/O Jack, Dundas, Ontario. Age 22
Thorpe, P/O Gordon, Toronto, Ontario.'Age 21
Topping, P/O Frederick, Prince Albert, Sask Age 23
Toppings, F/O Irving, Inchkeith, Saskatchewan. Age 23
Torbet, F/Sgt George, Halifax, Nova Scotia. Age 22
Uyen, F/O William, London, Ontario. Age 23
Van Fleet, F/O Ralph, Hamilton, Ontario. Age 20
Vaughan, Sgt John, Windsor Junction, N.S. Age 21
Weller, F/O Richard, Woodfire, B.C. Age 22
Wey, P/O Edward, Vancouver, B.C. Age 29
White, F/O Robert, Perth, Ontario. Age 26
Wilson, W.O. Raymond, Peachland, B.C. Age 22
Wilson, F/O James, Moose Jaw, Saskatchewan. Age 21
Zulauf, F/O Franklin, Milverton, Ontario. Age 23